To Finally See Clearly Now

Sofia Bances

BookLeaf
Publishing

India | USA | UK

Presentation by *BookLeaf Publishing*

Web: www.bookleafpub.com

E-mail: info@bookleafpub.com

ISBN: 9789360948559

First edition 2024

*To the younger version of myself, you've more
than earned it.*

ACKNOWLEDGEMENT

This second project of mine was no less exciting than the first, but it was also harder, given my happiness with the first. I have many people to thank for this opportunity. Most importantly, I'd like to yet again thank my father, Paul Bances. He taught me that all art has its beauty. I would've stopped writing a long- very long time ago if it wasn't for his support. Secondly, I'd like to thank Mrs. Lyann Aquino for I would've never started writing if it weren't for her. My mother also has helped me grow as a writer and inspired me to write honestly and authentically. My greatest supporter is and will always be my dad. I am beyond grateful for his companionship in this lifetime. He not only instilled in me but showed me the power of an incredible work ethic and dedication.

I'd love to thank BookLeaf as well for giving me this amazing opportunity. Finally, I'd also like to thank myself, I always had the opportunity to give up on myself and have considered it countless times, but as my father has always taught me- dreams without hard work and perseverance stay just that. Dreams.

PREFACE

Why do we read? What do we look for when we read? Whenever we read, we hope to feel something. To be enticed by the words on the page, to find a mirror of some kind, see ourselves on the page. For that reason, these poems can't be made without a little truth. Our ability to feel and recognize feeling in other settings is often what it means to be human. The good and the bad, the ups and the downs. These works are about exactly that, those feelings and thoughts behind the human mind. The ebbs and flows of motivation, the seventh circle of damnation where a self esteem may reside, and the weight of the light realization of ones own mortality. These poems are a work of self reflection, let's say. I learned to channel myself through my pen and see the shape of how I felt and who I was within the margins of the pages simply because I knew I couldn't do that verbally. Here are all the things that I couldn't say out loud or perhaps the things I told myself too many times. Since these are more personal, the poems do not tie together to form a cohesive story. I have chosen to share this with you, my audience. So thank you, reader. I hope somewhere within these lines of writing, yet

again, you can find a glimpse of yourself. You
hold the lens I used to see myself more clearly.

Quick Fix

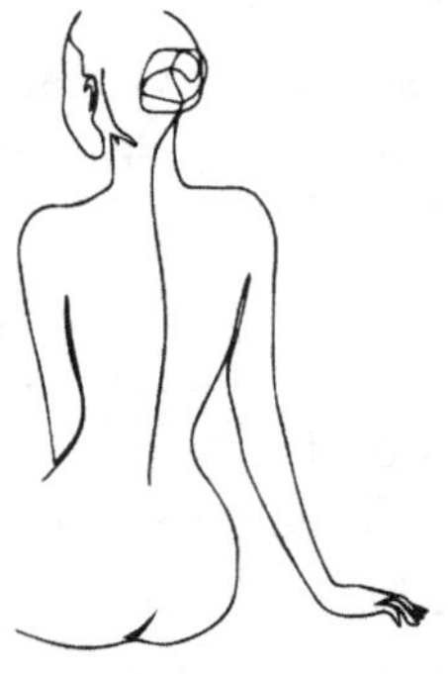

If I asked you to fix me,
Would you?
If you found me a new way to be,
Could you still call it "me"?

If I asked you to free me, you'd do it in an
instant.
But asked to fix me, your response is distant.
You say you can't fix what's not broken.
My cracks are nonexistent and change is
inconsistent, yet nonetheless I am insistent.

Fix me.
Make what's broken whole.
I know it's not free,
But it's not a heavy toll.
Just the me you thought you'd see.

That me that you knew.
Like Icarus, that soul flew.
Too high to the sun but not for arrogance.
But it tumbled down to Hades with pure
inelegance.

That soul went to the sun, not for arrogance,
But to find comfort in its heated bliss.
The poor thing was cold and empty when the
frostbite creeped in.
It made cracks on this vessel and tainted it with
its bitter sin.
The soul escaped.
Only to meet its inevitable fate.

That me that you once knew?
It's been buried beneath you.
But the cracks on this vessel remain.
Fixed, another soul this could maintain.

So if I asked you to fix me,
Would you?

You look like someone I once knew.
Someone who'd think the sun would be good to
pursue.

Lost in Someone Else

I've always been too worried about what
someone else needed.
I'd always disregard myself, regardless of how
hard my heart pleaded.
The joy I should've festered in myself, I
provided for others.
Because what is a single boy to an army of
brothers?
What does it matter what I do to make me happy
and how I feel?
Because the masses are now pleased and I'm
able to make my appeal.

Is it because it feels selfish? To make myself
happy?

Because when I stop pleasing others, everyone
gets so snappy.
It's not that I've given up and want to stop trying
I just need some for myself, so I can give more
without dying.

Asking you for the minimum seemed so
unreasonable,
But me giving you everything is so feasible?
That's not fair, but what did I expect?
I'm running nonstop and every chance to pause I
reject.
If I slow down now, I won't sprint to the finish.
If I pull back to breathe, my strength will
diminish.

This is unsustainable. My remaining power is
strainable.
This is so draining, this never ending training.
I'm so lost in someone else, I forget to save
myself.
There's gotta be a reason why,
Something buried deep in my mind.

If I always look out for you, then who's looking
out for me?
No one is there when my reflection wants to
scream.
Thinking about it now, everything is clearer.

I am always trying to be there for you,
But by the time I'm back in front of the mirror,
I'm looking at someone new.

New Director

They say you're the director of your life,
Well this movie of mine isn't quite right.
It's like a romcom, but there's no music, no set,
no plot, no rom, and no com-
It's just there.
Insignificant, like a rogue strand of hair.
Someone call Bridget Jones to save the movie,
Anything that might make me alive and "move
me".
No Chris Nolan, I have enough questions.
It's not Inception, there's no exceptions.
No Tarantino, I don't expect it to be that good.
Just enough that someone would like it,
hopefully I would.
Maybe Coppola!...I just like Godfather,
But a life like that won't get much farther.

Maybe I've just got lost in translation.
A miscommunication ending in damnation.
Even for a drama this is bad,
What happened to all the production value we
had?
Pick a genre so I know how this should go!
This is worse than any reality television show.
Maybe it's the lighting!
Maybe it's the sound!
Maybe it's the angles!
The plot!
The characters!
The themes!
The locations!
Please.
Give.
Me.
Something.

No… it's me. I need to be replaced.
I lack stability, this story is all over the place.
I'm not the protagonist in my own story.
I'm ridding my life of its glory.
The problem is my actors and director- and
that's me.
I'm not good enough to be my own lead!
I'm too incompetent of a director.
I belong in a less valuable sector.

If I don't know how to tell my story,
Then why should I tell it at all?

Someone call Rob Reines, because
When Harry Met Sally is looking a lot like
When misery met failure.

Limbo

Life has its ups and its downs,
But it mostly consists of its middles.
It's this period of nothingness that plagues your
mind with riddles.
It keeps you up, wondering why you aren't at an
up and how far are you from a down?
Like when you look at a lake, if I jump will it be
shallow or so deep I drown?
How are you supposed to know if it's safe to go?
How can I pull myself back up when everything
in me is telling me "no".
No you can't. No you shouldn't.
No, because when you were up there and asked
to stay, you couldn't.

Balance on that tightrope, careful as to which
side you'll sway.

Balance on that tightrope, stay in that limbo to
see another day.
You don't know which side takes you down or
pulls you up.
So don't test your luck. Admit that you're stuck.
Live in that limbo.
Or that way down will hurt, real slow.

Maybe it's the stoic in me.
I can live in this in-between.
This is nothing I haven't seen.
It makes the quick leaps into the air, almost
heavenly.
It makes the small swoops down, remind me to
stay afloat for my wellbeing.

Everything is more special, because you live in
the middle.
Perhaps that's the answer to life's riddle.
Bending backwards, with precarious balance,
under the pole.
Careful not to hit the ground, nor get too close to
the sun, safe in this little self made, median hole.

Balance on that tightrope.
It's the only tool that life gives you to cope.

A Quiet Desperation

So many words left unsaid,
With all these thoughts coursing through my
head,
So many things I want to ask
But the words leave with a swing of an axe,

A blade so sharp and bitter with tone,
Make my needs shrivel up alone.
I look in the mirror and in my eyes I see
The madness built up forces a shake from my
knees,

What have I become?
Who will I be?
If I can't simply ask for what I need?

So many walls I need to break through,
Yet my mind yells: "Your only barrier is you."

Why must my cries be so silent?
While in my mind- my craves are violent.
Just a simple request is all I ask,
Yet I cannot complete that simple task.

I will suffer in silence,
And perservere through violence.
My ailment is not permanent I suppose,
But my shackles are self-imposed.

The mirror cracks as my voice shakes,
Anticlimacticly, my shield breaks.
My stifled cries begin to slowly drown out,
As the ephemeral nature of my suffering is filled
with doubt.

Dear Younger Me,

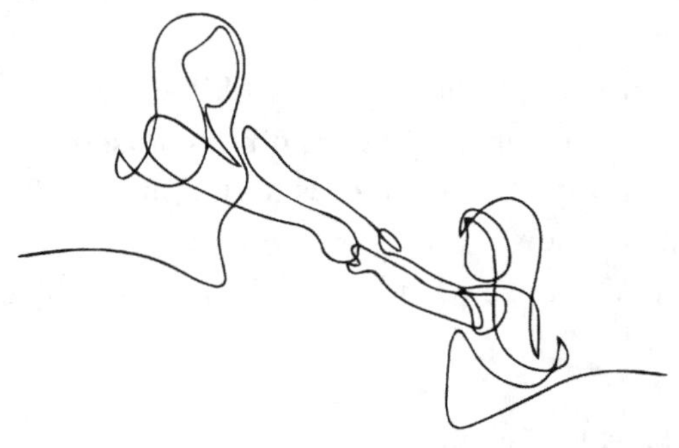

If I had to apologize to anyone, it would be you.
The younger me, the personification of my
youth.
Looking back, there are so many things I wish I
knew.
Things I could've used to protect and nurture
you.
I didn't let you cultivate that wonder, let you
dream.
I imposed reality and made you march upstream.

Perhaps I killed you, sliced you in our sleep?
Left the body on the floor, for my conscience to
sweep.
I didn't mean for us to grow up so fast.
I wouldn't have done it if I didn't think you'd
last.

I became the very thing I wanted to protect you
from.
I am the enemy, playing rudiments on his warm
drum.
I mourn you, because I know I killed you.
I killed what made you up, if not yourself.
I tore away at all the pieces until it made
someone new.
Then displayed what I had left, like a trophy on
a shelf.

Perhaps I failed you.
If you saw me now, what would you say?
The dreams that you had that I made true are
few,
Yet I can't even remember what they were,
They continue to escape by the day.
I use the puzzle pieces I have and try to infer,
But in the midst of it all, they get lost in the fray.

I should try to repair you, return the pieces I
stole.
The pieces I used to replace you, my misguided
goal.
Trying to grow up, trying to kill those dreams,
Now, that wonder is so dry, it rips at the seams.
If I was a smart person, I'd reteach you to walk.
But all I know is how to stifle you, treat you like
an existence to mock.

If you reached your feet, I'd push you to crawl.
I'd never let you even imagine getting it at all.

I pushed you away, because I was ashamed.
But I'm ashamed that I did that, now I'm afraid.
I wanted to be someone I'd be proud of.
But instead…
I'm sorry.

Ghost and the Songbird

The never ending story of the ghost and the
songbird.
I am both. I am a ghost of who I was and a
songbird who flew too far away.
He is both. He is a songbird whose songs I could
listen to all day and a ghost whose memory
won't fade away.

But I don't know if either of us will ever be
alright. Not completely.
But Casper the friendly ghost misses its canary
who would sing so sweetly.
Poor phantom doesn't understand why it ever
stopped cheeping and chirping, or why it had to
go.
But this ghost is ready for this songbird,
whenever it decides to fly home.

The ghost and the songbird, a story so old.
A story that's so classic it needs to be told.
When the bird would stop singing and the ghost
hold the poor thing in its phantom hands…
The ghost would say the words that no one else
would appreciate and understand:
How are you? Genuinely and authentically? In
sincerity and curiosity? In serenity and
calamity?
Will you fly towards the sun, sweet Icarus?
Or will you stay in my cold dead hands, just like
this?

But I don't know if either of us will ever be
alright. Not completely.
But Casper the friendly ghost misses its canary
who would sing so sweetly.
The ghost and the songbird, the corpse and the
raven.
A story that since then, I've always been cravin'.
Something similar but just not it.
Something close enough, but the ghost and the
songbird is a piece in a puzzle that just doesn't
quite fit.

Will you fly towards the sun, sweet Icarus?
Or will you stay in my cold dead hands, just like
this?
Either way the songbird will die.

The cold won't warm its wings.
Or it will go too close to the sky.
That's just the way of these things.

But I don't know if either of us will ever be
alright. Not completely.
But Casper the friendly ghost misses its canary
who would sing so sweetly.
Poor phantom doesn't understand why it ever
stopped cheeping and chirping, or why it had to
go.
But this ghost is ready for this songbird,
whenever it decides to fly home.

A Misery In My Soul

Maybe I was just made wrong.
There's something fundamentally mismatched in
my body.
My voice is off key in the tune of my life's song.
My hair's made straight by life but naturally it's
knotty.

Nothing is as it should be.
Everything's a facade, a persona of who I should
be.
Every action is calculated for the result it should
return.
Every favor is calculated for the debt I should
return.

I pay the pauper in my mind every single day,
with no pence left to save.
I work nonstop to lessen my neverending debt,
turning myself into my own slave.
What's the purpose? What's the point?
I'm just a puppet, locked at every joint.

This isn't to say that I'm ashamed,
Nor is it to say that I am to be blamed.
I'm just trapped in the jail of my brain,
Yet every day I'm locked up is another day
closer to insane.
Naturally, I'm in solitary, serving my sentence
alone.
But the number of guards, keeping me at bay,
surely has grown.

They beat me down, day by day.
Once they get bored of one method, they find
another way.
Another way to keep me small, make me no
threat at all.
Another way to keep me locked up in my cell,
all by my self.

This is the misery that's held in my soul.
This is the misery that they cannot risk being
freed.
Hiding this misery is the warden's ultimate goal.

But wanting to kill it is the result of the warden's
greed.

I was just made wrong, down to the parts that
make me whole.
I am trapped because I'm wrong, down to the
level of my soul.

The Music

Symphonies entail the most elegant of melodies.
All the dissonances lead to perfect remedies.
Some pieces have movements, parts that
connect.
It's a sound that flows, like life, except…
Like life, each piece, each movement must
conclude.
Thus, I'm pretty sure I'm screwed.

It's like American Pie, but my flute stays clean.
This music has such a score, I dont know what
the notes mean.
The melody seems nice though,
It's not quite my tempo.

The first movement is slow and nice,
The second is faster with some spice,

The third is full of staccato but the melody
persists,
The final is quiet and cut short as the conductor
insists.

What's done is done and quickly as it ended, the
writing of a new symphony has begun.
But as it was for the last one, the final result is
none.
All I know, is that the players in this concert
really tried.
And with that, today, the music died.

Who I Wanted To Be

Who am I?
When I was young I wanted to be an astronomer,
I was obsessed with the night sky.
Then instead I wanted to be a philosopher, see
through the matrix not through my eye.
I decided on neither, because I realized they
weren't needed.
Who am I? I hope I'm not unneeded too.
Then I said I wanted to be a writer! But I have
no good story to tell.
It's just me throwing a pity party and I'm not
even doing it well!

I don't have to know everything immediately,
As long as when I do, everything's organized
neatly.
I may not be needed.

But maybe I'm wanted?
My own hateful thoughts, I feeded.
By my own memories, I'm haunted.
Warnings that should've been heeded,
Self deprecation that shouldn't have been
taunted.

The things I wanted to be are already out of
time…
So who's to say I'm not out of mine?

It's hard to know that you could never be what
you want,
Especially when you haven't been able to be
anything yet.
But this is the perception of the situation I
already have set.
It no longer matters who I become,
Because my work will never be done.
And though I wished to be a dreamer, I'll never
be one.

I'll take the consolation prize that I am,
Hopefully I'll make the most of it, but
sometimes? I frankly don't give a damn.

New Year

Resolutions mean change.
Everybody wants to improve.
Some people can't catch up.
Going through the motions is all you can do.
Little by little the pressure to "reinvent" builds
up.
"New year new me" isn't real.
There's so much excitement that I'm meant to,
but still don't feel.
It wouldn't matter if it was September
Only that we change the number at the end of
December.
Now, the thing is, I'm expected to be someone
better.

The number I put at the end of the date
Doesn't tell me who I am at the end of the day.
I don't care for your resolutions or diets.
That's your bullshit, I'm sure there's someone
else who'll buy it.
New year deep cleaning seems more useful
When the spring pollen infests and infects your
home.
Lifestyle changes to seem more youthful
Do it when you feel a day too old.
The tail end of December shouldn't tell you a
thing.
It's just like last year, what do you think it'll
bring?
What does it matter?

That's the funny thing. It doesn't.
It's just a pattern that cycles.
Like a dog chasing a tail.
Forever in circles but nothing will change.
Many people get depressed on this day.
"It's the end of an era" they all say.
This is to reflect on the past
And plan for the future, coming at you fast.

But that's not the problem.
That's not its purpose.

You're worried about a change and ending that
isn't coming.
A circle has no beginning or end, it continues
running.

So run.
Like you're the number of the year, you run.
Until you forget what you're running from.
Then comes January 4th.
Just like that, what were those resolutions
worth?
Oh right. Nothing.

Because a number doesn't change a thing.
It's just the pressure to improve that the new
years enjoys to bring.

Countdown

Life is a precious thing that all take for granted. I am no exception. Everyone tries to live their life thinking they'll never die. Then there's the few who live knowing the countdown, the ticking timebomb of their heartbeat. The idiot between the two groups is unclear. There is enjoyment in living without fear of the end but there is also wisdom in living in no time other than the present.

Learn to be both of these people. Either way, hopefully, when the ticking stops, you'll see that you already had lived a life that is so beautifully and undeniably genuine and you.

I'm scared. What if the bomb goes off too early?
What if the blast is too quick? Or worse, what if
it's something that I wasn't good enough to fix?

Tick tock, I'm running out of time,
Tick tock, that clock just won't shut up!

I've never felt free.
Have you ever been so happy that you feel like
you can fly?
I want to live my life like I'll never die…
I want to be able to throw my arms back, yell
into the sky.

I want to fall and not care if anyone catches me.
Because the clock still ticks,
But there's so many opportunities I can miss,
This one I can't resist.

The grim reaper approaches,
With a scythe in hand.
He comes to glean my soul,
He makes one demand.

"The clock has struck midnight.
Make your case.
Put up a fight.
Just in case,

I change my mind and give you just a little more
time."

The ultimate countdown and one final chance.
My pounding heartbeat will promise me one
final dance.

Tick tock, I am running out of time.
But there's enough for me to live like I'll never
die
I wait for the reaper, with, his scythe in hand.
He has not returned and I don't understand.

Now I understand, why the clock won't stop its
chime.
He wants me to beg, beg to run out of time.
But if I can live like I'll never die,
Ignorance is bliss, I'll yell into the sky

My heart counts down until it's too broken to
fix.
But I hear it now, the clocks unwavering ticks.
He waits for me to run out of time,
When I give up and let the clock stop its chime.
Living like I'll never die and he thinks I'm done.
But I have asthma and I hate to run.

A Writer's Love

Dear pen and paper,
Have I ever told you that I love you?
Have I told you that you always know the right
thing to say?
You do what you do and I don't know what it is,
but you do it the right way!
You make me feel loved in a way that I thought I
didn't deserve.
Through our journey, you manage to surprise me
at every turn.
I wish I knew what to say.
I wish there was a simple and easy way.
But there's no true way to encapsulate
The way you crumbled my walls and opened the
gate.
But I doubt you understand the weight,
Or the importance that you taught me to be my
own soulmate.

A kind regard,
Your Poetic Wild Card.

I'm excited to hear your reply!
I'll write a letter back, write it every time!
Word to the wise,
Soon you'll realize,
The words on paper that we write,
Are for people to see our love in another life.

A Scarlet Letter

Everyone's heard of a scarlet letter,
A classic story sure, but one you'd expect to be
better.
A love that taunts and haunts both night and day,
A final breath of yours, that unlike your
memory, simply faded away.

Here's my scarlet letter to you,
As Katy Perry would call my "one who got
away"
I wish here written was something new,
But your voice is still what haunts me at the end
of the day.
I know it shouldn't be like this.
I remember when I used to reach for your hand,
Now it's like the Sistine chapel where I just
miss.
I can't imagine a good person could understand.

I hate this feeling,

The anxiety alone has me reeling,
I thought I was better than this,
But the past has proven to be hard to dismiss,
What if everyone was right?
What if I'm the one that's wrong, was never
alright?
Maybe I was crazy, maybe it was a coincidence?
Maybe it was a conspiracy of a badly-timed
unrelated incidence?

Either way, I'm sorry.
Either way, I wish you were here.
Either way, it doesn't matter that I crave for you
to be near.
Because either way, it's too late.
I should end this scarlet letter here,
Hide my secrets and confessions under a wax
seal.
Or maybe I should have you read it, for me to
hear…

I'd hear your voice break under the betrayal, I'd
hear it shake from the shock, I'd hear your
crumple it in your fist, and I'd hear your scared
breathing under this intense gaze I wouldn't be
able to resist!

How could I do this to myself, not even to you?
I've given these thoughts so much to consume.

But nonetheless here's my scarlet letter to you,
Surely you remember what this means.
You can read between the lines and through the
seams,

I used to use paper for the things my mouth
couldn't do,
It would express my love, my care and devotion
to you.

So here's the scarlet letter.
The one I wrote for you.
I thought I was someone better.
You're too good a muse to pick someone new.
I will wrap the envelope under my mourning
veil,
Because as much as I try to forget you, I know
I'll always fail.

Let Me Go

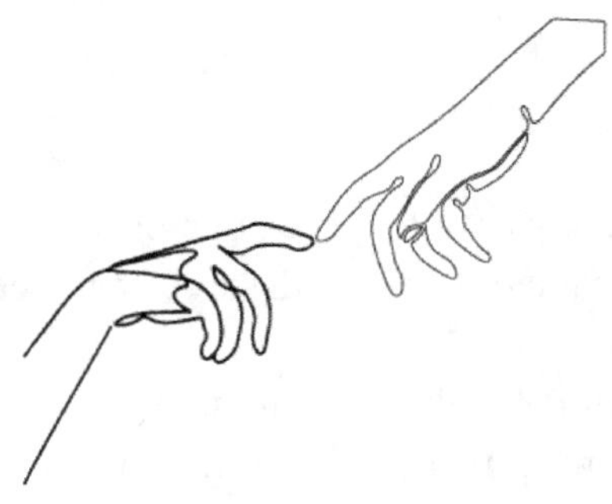

I'm afraid I've lost myself. But I also refuse to
let her go.
Like her body's trapped inside me, and I'm now
somebody I'll never know.
I'm in the shadow of who I once remembered
being.
But whatever I brought to the table before, I
know I'm no longer bringing.
I could flourish and thrive if I just let myself be.
Not who everyone wants, but whoever is
actually me.

A cage made of gold is still a cage.
I'm trapped by the margins on my page.
A trap instilled by my mind that I'm trapped
inside is still a trap,

The key to this lock is hidden in the part of my
mind that I can't yet tap.
I grasp for the feeling or the instinct to escape,
But against my prison bars, my nails can only
scrape.

Scrape away until they've gone brittle,
Not the bars, only my nails have been beaten
little.
Every effort I make is for nought,
Because what I was fighting for, even I forgot.
I could fly, but instead I'd drown,
Because the weight of my memories pulls me
down.

In the reflection of the ocean below,
I see her staring back at me.
The light in those eyes, those memories I see.
She nods and I wonder if her heart would break,
If I were to shake off this weight.

Maybe I don't but I'm sure she'd know,
That it's probably for the best if I let us go.

I Didn't Ask to Be This Way

I don't know why everything I do is wrong.
It's not like I'm trying to be bad?
I'm making every effort I can, proving everyone
different,
And shouldering every challenge that can be
thrown at a man, keeping that facade, smile
consistent.
I don't know what it takes to do right by you. By
anyone.
I don't even know what is right by me anymore.
I'm too caught up trying to kill that girl inside
me. The girl that was wrote off as everything
wrong with humanity. The "monster" inside of
me.

I don't know what it is about her that's so bad.

I've tried to figure it out, spent my whole life,
But what point from hearing it every second of
every day, do you start to believe it too?
"No, stop being selfish. No, you can't be
redeemed. No, you can't change. You don't
deserve it. It's not possibly in your nature. You
couldn't handle being good. It's not you."

But I don't even know what I am.
I haven't had the chance to be anything.
But by the time I could open my eyes, I was
already making mistakes.
I haven't had the chance to be anything because
I've been too busy trying not to be what you say
I am. What everyone says I am.
I'm not anything or anyone in particular, but I'm
not that person I was told I was.

I didn't ask to be a bad person.
I didn't ask to be made broken.
I didn't ask for this.
I've got a high card "3" and I'm still expected to
win this hand?
I didn't ask to be made wrong.
Incapable of doing any right.

I don't know why I thought I could prove
anything other than what they already say.
I don't know why I thought I could change.

Because I still don't know what it was I was
meant to change.

I know deep down that they're wrong about me.
But I've believed them since the beginning of
time.
When I look in the mirror, their version of me is
the one that I see.
I've snuffed the flame of any version that's
mine.

I didn't ask to be this way.
But no matter how hard I try,
I can't escape that this is my only way to be.

Won't Be Long Now

I blame you for everything that's wrong with me
and my life.
But I never gave you credit for what it was that
got us this far.
Because of you, we never are average, because
we set the bar.
Maybe I shouldn't put you to the knife,
Instead I should bring you to light.
There's no real purpose in this fight.
I need you and I can't refute that, try as I might.

I'm sorry.
I'm sorry for all the yelling and the abuse,
I'm sorry for only seeing your flaws and being
so obtuse.
I didn't mean to break every mirror in this maze,
I just couldn't stand to meet your- well my own
gaze.

Atlas cannot crumble under the weight of the
sky,
For everyone will remember that he fell in the
end,
Not that he managed to be so strong.
I only noticed when the light went out, not that it
was on for so long.

I'll give you credit from now on,
Because I'm nothing once you're gone.
We are one and the same,
I'll be sure to nurture your flame.
Until we go ablaze and the light stays bright,
Until Icarus's wings take flight.
Only we won't fall.
We will simply have it all.
The weight, the sky,
The light, and all hidden in our eye.

I'll give it all to you and though I'm not exactly
sure how,
I know that it won't be long now.

Heal Me With Your Hope

A common theme in every tale.
Shows how the hero will always prevail.
Breaking through barriers- with such elegance
and grace
Never without a shining smile on their face

Each fable, folktale, and story is told
With the foundations of the rebellions left alone
With the light of those who've lost
Crossing lanes that others fear to cross

With the arrival of a new day
And the smiles of those finding their way
Comes the relief of battles past
As the time moves on too fast
After all is lost and all is done
The stirring feeling has finally begun

It erupts as it crashes down
Heals the heart's wounds bleeding out

The base of success
A gift to the blessed
Closes the door
To be relieved once more.

I see it now, the key to my success.
The key is within me, I must confess.
I found sanctuary within my own soul.
This is how I'll heal.
I recovered what it was that my own mind stole.
Now I have something that no one else can steal.

I will make peace between my past and my
present.
I won't think you evil as I once used to.
It'll soon be easy but for now, it's unpleasant.
This is a mix of feelings, good but no less new.

This is the feeling of the loosening of a rope.
This is the soliloquy of someone who's
discovered hope.

Cliffs

There are two types of people in this world;
Those who die on hills and those who live
jumping off cliffs.
I refuse to drown in inch deep valleys.
I will not waste away in currents that don't drift.
This is why I ask, if you would be willing to
jump off this cliff.

Take the risk and enjoy the spoils,
Or burn with regret as your blood boils.
Surely it'll be worth it, but that you don't yet
know,

But you'll never figure it out if you don't give it
a go.
If you hesitate, you will drown in only a glass of
water,
Whereas I will bathe in the ocean like a free sea
otter.

I will leap and I must take you with me for all
the things you refuse to see.
You will hold yourself back and take me down
with you and I'll never be who I'm meant to be.
Jump with me and together we will manifest our
gills,
Because if not, how else will we experience new
thrills?

I can search flat lands as much as one could
want.
But what kind of things would you find to
flaunt?
The horizon is as flat as the lands you pursue,
Therefore you wouldn't discover anything new.

Why display such cowardice when searching for
your character?
Is it a reflection of what it is that you're too
scared to find?
Or is it just laziness, that there's no depth to
what you have inside?

Know My Name

I work too hard to lose it all when I die.
I hope that by that time I've done enough to let
my soul fly.
Sure, I'm taking a loan on life and death is my
fine.
There's so many famous names, who will
remember mine?

I used to want a nom d'plume as I used to hate
my name,
My first was too common, my last was too rare,
But by the time for my alias came, I realized that
I didn't care.
I take pride in the name that defines me.
It represents all I've been and all I will be.
It's all that I've accomplished and the
accomplishments I've yet to see.

It belongs to my family, one I'm proud to be part
of.
I'll wear it even once I've flown from the nest,
like a wedding dove.
This name is mine and I've learned to own it.
And I'll keep it clean, regardless of where
you've thrown it.

Hopefully by the end of this page,
I've freed myself from my own cage.
I've taken back my youth, I've taken back my
memories.
I learned to love myself and indulge in my old
reveries.

Though things have changed, the person I am is
still the same.
I pushed away and fought with every spark I'd
ignite,
I fuelled enough fires in my soul to light up the
night.
I hated myself enough to know what strength
lies behind the one who bears this name.
Even under a pseudonym, regardless of the
celebrity, there's a person under that power and
fame.
Tell me, even with no pen name, power, or fame,
would you still remember who I was?

Would you remember how hard I worked
regardless of cause?
You'd only remember if it was a result of who I
became,
But I know myself enough to know now, that
You'd
Know
My
Name.

I Can See You Now

Looking in the mirror now,
I see something new but I don't know how.
For the first time, I can truly see my reflection.
Everyone should deserve to love themselves and
I'm no exception.

I see you now, the me that I hid away.
Let me hold you close and assure you it's okay.
I'll hold your hand and guide you along,
Quell the fears in your mind with a comforting
song.

Everytime someone tries to get under my skin,
I'm reminded of you.

Everything they can say, I'll already yelled to
this mirror,
Hoping the relection's clearer,
When I yell something new.
After everything I shared, because I never cared,
You're not too badly impaired and maybe you
don't need to be repaired.

You're not broken, you don't need fixing.
I see that you're just seasoned with struggle and
need a bit of mixing.
I can see you for who we are.
I'm shocked you're so close, I thought I pushed
you so far.
Near enough for me to grasp with a desperate
hand.
Ready for me to take you home once we land.